W0010193

AMERICAN ZERO

STELLA WONG

Winner of the 2018 Two Sylvias Press Chapbook Prize

Two Sylvias Press

Copyright © 2019 Stella Wong

All rights reserved. No part of this book may be reproduced in any form without the written permission of the publisher, except for brief quotations embodied in critical articles and reviews.

Two Sylvias Press
PO Box 1524
Kingston, WA 98346
twosylviaspress@gmail.com

Cover Photo Credit: Elaine Dong
Cover Design: Kelli Russell Agodon
Book Design: Annette Spaulding-Convy
Author Photo: Stella Wong
Contest Judge: Danez Smith

Created with the belief that great writing is good for the world, Two Sylvias Press mixes modern technology, classic style, and literary intellect with an eco-friendly heart. We draw our inspiration from the poetic literary talent of Sylvia Plath and the editorial business sense of Sylvia Beach. We are an independent press dedicated to publishing the exceptional voices of writers.

For more information about Two Sylvias Press please visit:
www.twosylviaspress.com

First Edition. Created in the United States of America.

ISBN: 978-1-948767-08-8

Two Sylvias Press
www.twosylviaspress.com

Praise for *American Zero*

Stella Wong wields the kind of weaponry I live to be slayed by. Funny as hell, delightfully strange and full of a sneaky and giant heart, *American Zero* is holds its beloved subjects – friends, siblings, Lucy Liu, grapefruits, all the jesuses the poet can muster – and gives them body with wicked imagination and knock-out tenderness. This book will knock the windows of your heart not just open, but out the frame once you see how far Wong can dive into fear and the terrible possibles of humanness can still carry back something like hope, gooder than joy. Wong has crafted a brief, but mighty collection of poems that point towards the bright possibly of power to make us better dreamers, better lovers, better homies, and oh my jesuses how thankful I am for this abundant offering. I'm sure you will be too. —**Danez Smith** (Contest Judge)

જી

If poetry were a biathlon, Stella Wong would take the gold. She's a solid skier and a crack shot, each poem a bullet hitting its mark. Thank God she's turned all of this energy and accuracy into poetry. 'Where do you put your body of color' she asks. Then proceeds to school everyone. Stella Wong is a force, a maker, a master. —**D.A. Powell**

જી

Bookended by dramatic appeals to Lucy Liu and America itself, another name for Stella Wong's exciting, candid, incantatory American Zero might be "American Presence," for Wong's is a crisp new voice intently, intensely, undeniably zeroing in, and it's certainly not for nothing that the important last word of the important last poem is "here." —**Robyn Schiff**

જી

You and Stella Wong are the last two people on Earth. You're going to witness her "ride in/to hell" and you will need to prepare yourself for the moment when she decides to use her "daddy voice" on Jesus. You're the last two people on Earth because the truth—the truth of Stella Wong's voice, the truth of these poems—has scared away the timid. But be strong. The apocalypse of *American Zero* is scary and dangerous, yes, but it's also a lot of fun. —**Josh Bell**

Acknowledgements

Much thanks to the editors and readers of the following publications, where the following poems were first accepted, many in earlier versions:

Narrative: "Pineapple"

Cortland Review: "Who'd rob god?" and "One child policy is the
                                party pickup line"

Colorado Review: "Pomelo" and "Everything about you is offensive
                                except your cat"

BOAAT: "Bandaids didn't make a color for me, or Thinking inside the box,
        or Crayon within the lines"

Tupelo Quarterly: "Halloween Redux"

This book is for the women of my family: my mother—my first mentor and my eternal muse, my aunts, and my grandmother.

All my gratitude to my teachers Doug Powell, Jim Galvin, Robyn Schiff, Jorie Graham, Josh Bell, Ju Yon Kim, Golda Vainberg-Tatz, and the heart of Iowa, Sam Chang and Connie Brothers.

All my love to moi brand Jason and Priyanka, my cheerleader Darara, Esteban, my dear reader Jack, my photographer Sam, and multitalented Elaine.

All my thanks to Danez Smith and the editors at Two Sylvias for believing in this manuscript, and the editors of the journals in which some of the poems have previously appeared: *Narrative, Tupelo Quarterly, Cortland Review, Colorado Review* and *BOAAT*.

Table of Contents

Pineapple

Lucy Liu, don't worry,
I remember you
from the movie
Chicago, where
Richard Gere said
your mother owned all
the pineapples
of Hawaii, because
of course
with a surname of Baxter
you'd be an American
Kitty, bastardized roots
for this yellow fruit.
You'd be the most far-out
almost foreign
villain/villanelle, sweet
heart of America. I wonder
if, in addition to kneeing
two guys, you felt something break
your mother's heart, captured
in your sights
the faces of the men and women of
America, cheating on
the imperiled overrich.
You teach me how to act
imperial. Overreach.
Act as if gold
medalled, first
prized for what
lines you land,
which marks you flay.
Lucy Liu, you are no
dragging lady
of the spouse.
Sidekick,
take the addict

and make a detective
out of Sherlock.
Joan Watson,
you are koan
and kingmaker
and go on
not as an
Othered best friend
but as a game-changer.
Also Lucy Liu,
you are good
at being the head
of a crime ring.
Lucy Liu, you've had
no real need
to keep
a ring of men around
you. O-Ren,
they're dead
meat, as you see
the white woman
in a yellow skin-
tight suit
can really pick them
off, easy. You're the hit
list's top billing.
When she beheads you,
plant your crown.
Your trunk will grow back
where you went down.
You show me
I can come
to fruition
and yellow on my own
terms.
Lucy Liu, do not stay
silent—this is not
an old black-and-
white. You are well

within your rights.
You can feel free
to be bad,
and reel
me in.
If you can act, then
I can act out.
This is not your death
scene. You can afford
to take the heads off
everyone in the room,
and not leave them in
one piece. If they will
remember you for your murder
why not make a killing.

Halloween

We do not buy
into crystals, poker

chips or other forms of bread
and circuses. We made ourselves up

in the mirror laced with rosary
and Mardi Gras beads, stranded

without the definition of fairy
lights, refusing to name ourselves
nympho, klepto, pyro.

We cannot afford the goose, cold
and blue & snow-white,

preferring to take it straight
from the mouth

of the next-door come-as-eurotrash party,
smoking the birthday boy out
of his self-imported cigarettes.

This is what I believe in:
my roommate's prayer-soft blanket

pleated in turquoise & other
shades of *please*. I believe we hail

voodoo utilized on ritualistic break-up,
one of us peeing on a pillow while
the other one pretends we cannot hear.

Let us pretend we are descended
from witches, have everything yet

to be maimed, too hot & too irregular to
live. I'll be your misshapen & your

mishaps will be mine, so scarce
and precious to be beloved. I see you,

hallowed queen folding sheets
some color other than white.

Who'd Rob God?

You break it you pay for it.

I'm so very bored with all my Jesuses today.
I already talked to them in a baby voice
and by them, I mean all of them
baby Jesuses I stole from Target.

I targeted each and every one—
I lifted them. I lifted them from the shelf.
Shoplifted? I'd rather not,
that word's no fun

at all. They were just, wow
so funny looking. You know how medieval babies
were really just full-size men, or how
cherubs are ambiguously sexed?

Maybe I'll talk to my Jesuses in my daddy voice next.

Pomelo

In my kitchen, some white man
        shouts, what is this? R tells him it's a pomelo,

interrogates the fruit, like the cops
        with Buddha

in custody, head
        old and wrinkled.

For my grandmother, held
        up—after the flight

home, after the funeral—
        in customs, has survived

much more than is custom to speak. Imported bride
        of little import.

When I head out for the pomelo,
        the fallen alien has landed

defaced, branded
        by fingernails, some cruel

curiosity of the bright.
        yellow hide carrying white man-

made mottles that look, in spite
        of the gossip that is not gospel,
            like dimples.

I carry my baby to the bar
        because I can't drink. Buddhist, I say,

or pregnant. A colonizer insists we split it,

carving the fruit into spheres of influence.
        What color is it? asks his girlfriend.

We're all pink on the inside. She almost chokes
        on her laughter

and no one realizes that
I am not talking about the meat.

Bandaids didn't make a color for me, or Thinking inside the box, or Crayon within the lines

A spell

Where do you put your body
of color

Where do you put
your body of color

Where do you put
your color of body

Where do you put
your off-color body

Where do you color
your body on

Where do you put off
your body

Where do you put
of your body

What do you color
of your body

Where do you body
your color

Where you off-put
you, there you are:

you are body.
You are color.

Everything About You is Offensive Except Your Cat

After "The Thousand-Hand Bodhisattva"

A pop singer populates
her songs with geishas, poplar-tall, all

stilts & prayer
hands & sexual.

Katy Perry, in time
I learned all things white

have their own rules: crazy turns
to eccentricity. Zealous to the elect.

Fetish to something
like respect.

Like her popularity, her yellowface
and Hello Kitty obsession will be

forgotten by the lucky cat's wave.
What is not lost: us double-exposed

shots with a blur
of wholly curious palms

and a curated summer playlist, held together
by Popsicle sticks & a prayer

to a goddess
who looks

nothing like their savior. What is more
sacred than

a thousand arms
born gold

like me,
dancing on

one hand,
playing

myself with
all the rest.

Halloween Redux

In my photo there you are
girl, where you going

wearing that Trojan
centurion helmet

& wielding a trash can
heavy-lidded.

We vow to never have sex
& our empire never goes down

on us like the past
empires. After a shot

which goes down smooth, you have
stuffed the embossed

helmet under your shirt,
as if smuggling his baby

robot dolls
is the closest to hugging

& likewise shiny gifts
as only you can get.

When we come to
you, lost, you tell us how

the doctor frames you
& we spin a webMD

diagnosis into fine compliment—
with bi-polar you've taken over

the whole world. How magnetic
you are, when you show off

your knees for the first time
forgiven by scars.

Let's toast to
us, the Last Triumvirate.

Your therapist has
eyes the exact shade of

vodka, never gives you a second shot
like we know how to do.

We know how to dance
to your maniac tune, stirring up

dust from the costume's
plumes. When we sneeze, you say you would

bless us but we've already been
with your presence, all disco, smoke &

three colognes. We are up
to our own devices, trumpeting

like Prometheus, what hell-colored
colonizer's hat we stole.

Let's be our own kings,
prom or drag.

If we're your other halves,
that makes you more than

holy—you,
in your photo, taken

after you admitted
us breaking

in the door—
you're half

somewhere
we don't know

beyond the frame. It is you
we are always in the process of winning

back, braced not by dagger nor bone
but the blood-red feathers

we carried back.

One child policy is the Party Pickup Line

There's an eagle that has
usually
one child.

If it has two it will choose
only
one to take

care of, & purposefully
mistreat the other
so it dies.

The bigger sibling pecks
the little one so he's more shitty
looking.

So the parents feed the bigger
one & they eventually ditch
the little one in the middle

of nowhere. So it dies.
And so it goes.
I would peck you now if I could.

Peck you on the cheek.
On the cheek until
the cheekbone was exposed.

I feel like you would look good
eating red Jello.
You know

red Jello is made out of gelatin,
bone?
I'll enjoy

15

my ride in
to hell now.

Next to all the writers from the Inquisition.

Prank-calling on Chatrooms on a Friday Night

It's our new normal
weekend appetite,

and dragonfly
blue mud-masked,

we choose camouflage, the prospect
of jail & prank-

calling on chatrooms.
We munch

on gold fortune
cookies with typos.

We can never tell
whose thirst is real when

we Scheherazades, underwritten
by schadenfreude, are so well-stocked.

Glutted
on some virgin floodlight, we are

unspent & spilling
without a reason to clean up

our acts. How quickly we give up
our real names so they give in to our lies.

We are desperate to know
them & what makes them come

to this site,
anonymous, pupils

dilated, waiting for some
connection to dial up.

Stella, name
of the classiest beer...

While we detox
our skin in firming, dead

sea clay, rich
with superpowers,

you reel
in the affirmations, fine-tuning

the punchline *I'm drunk*
on you right now.

Chameleon, cold-blooded
I lay it on

thick, I lie I am
a different color

of mouth, an older age.
We down the watery dregs

of some strange attention.
We are touched

by the blue glow of a new flame, not realizing
it's the hottest part.

In the face
of being unwanted for who we are,

we can still sell our masquerade
until we can't make out

who is left
on the board.

Afterwards, we wash our faces off,
form our foam

moustaches & cocoon
our baptized hair.

We are the fools
picking through the lures

of crushed fortune, clowning, climbing
back into our own

skins & baiting
the sure things back

from their drowning.

While I'm Not a Heroic Couplet

America, I am not a negative
nor a positive. I am your zero

sum game, what I take you take
as stolen from you. My life is to be had

for a song, free as
America. To you I am nothing

but a number, O gasp you are startled
I am still here. Oh a zero,

made by my Song ancestors
instead of leaving a space

on the page. J says,
it's American, not American't!

I disagree, it's the can as in trash,
I feel obliged to take myself out.

In time. America, I only wish
you would leave me

a space, at the very least
on paper, to sign.

I am still right
here.

Stella Wong is a poet with degrees from Harvard and the Iowa Writer's Workshop. Wong's poems have appeared or are forthcoming in *POETRY, Colorado Review, Missouri Review, Indiana Review, Cortland Review, Tupelo Quarterly, BOAAT, Narrative, Poetry Northwest*, and the *LA Review of Books*. She is the winner of the 2016 Academy of American Poets University Prize and the 2018 Two Sylvias Press Chapbook Prize judged by Danez Smith.

Publications by Two Sylvias Press:

The Daily Poet: Day-By-Day Prompts For Your Writing Practice
by Kelli Russell Agodon and Martha Silano (Print and eBook)

The Daily Poet Companion Journal (Print)

Fire On Her Tongue: An Anthology of Contemporary Women's Poetry
edited by Kelli Russell Agodon and Annette Spaulding-Convy (Print and eBook)

The Poet Tarot and Guidebook: A Deck Of Creative Exploration (Print)

American Zero, Winner of the 2018 Two Sylvias Press Chapbook Prize by Stella Wong (Print and eBook)

The Inspired Poet: Writing Exercises to Spark New Work (Print and eBook)
by Susan Landgraf

All Transparent Things Need Thundershirts, Winner of the 2017 Two Sylvias Press Wilder Prize by Dana Roeser (Print and eBook)

Where The Horse Takes Wing: The Uncollected Poems of Madeline DeFrees
edited by Anne McDuffie (Print and eBook)

In The House Of My Father, Winner of the 2017 Two Sylvias Press Chapbook Prize by Hiwot Adilow (Print and eBook)

Box, Winner of the 2017 Two Sylvias Press Poetry Prize
by Sue D. Burton (Print and eBook)

Tsigan: The Gypsy Poem (New Edition)
by Cecilia Woloch (Print and eBook)

PR For Poets
by Jeannine Hall Gailey (Print and eBook)

Appalachians Run Amok, Winner of the 2016 Two Sylvias Press Wilder Prize
by Adrian Blevins (Print and eBook)

Pass It On!
by Gloria J. McEwen Burgess (Print)

Killing Marias
by Claudia Castro Luna (Print and eBook)

The Ego and the Empiricist, Finalist 2016 Two Sylvias Press Chapbook Prize
by Derek Mong (Print and eBook)

The Authenticity Experiment
by Kate Carroll de Gutes (Print and eBook)

Mytheria, Finalist 2015 Two Sylvias Press Wilder Prize
by Molly Tenenbaum (Print and eBook)

Arab in Newsland , Winner of the 2016 Two Sylvias Press Chapbook Prize
by Lena Khalaf Tuffaha (Print and eBook)

The Blue Black Wet of Wood, Winner of the 2015 Two Sylvias Press Wilder Prize
by Carmen R. Gillespie (Print and eBook)

Fire Girl: Essays on India, America, and the In-Between
by Sayantani Dasgupta (Print and eBook)

Blood Song
by Michael Schmeltzer (Print and eBook)

Naming The No-Name Woman,
Winner of the 2015 Two Sylvias Press Chapbook Prize
by Jasmine An (Print and eBook)

Community Chest
by Natalie Serber (Print)

Phantom Son: A Mother's Story of Surrender
by Sharon Estill Taylor (Print and eBook)

What The Truth Tastes Like
by Martha Silano (Print and eBook)

landscape/heartbreak
by Michelle Peñaloza (Print and eBook)

Earth, Winner of the 2014 Two Sylvias Press Chapbook Prize
by Cecilia Woloch (Print and eBook)

The Cardiologist's Daughter
by Natasha Kochicheril Moni (Print and eBook)

She Returns to the Floating World
by Jeannine Hall Gailey (Print and eBook)

Hourglass Museum
by Kelli Russell Agodon (eBook)

Cloud Pharmacy
by Susan Rich (eBook)

Dear Alzheimer's: A Caregiver's Diary & Poems
by Esther Altshul Helfgott (eBook)

Listening to Mozart: Poems of Alzheimer's
by Esther Altshul Helfgott (eBook)

Crab Creek Review 30ᵗʰ Anniversary Issue featuring Northwest Poets edited by
Kelli Russell Agodon and Annette Spaulding-Convy (eBook)

Please visit Two Sylvias Press (www.twosylviaspress.com) for information on
purchasing our print books, eBooks, writing tools, and for submission guidelines
for our annual book prizes.

CPSIA information can be obtained
at www.ICGtesting.com
Printed in the USA
BVHW031458090820
585836BV00003B/263

9 781948 767088